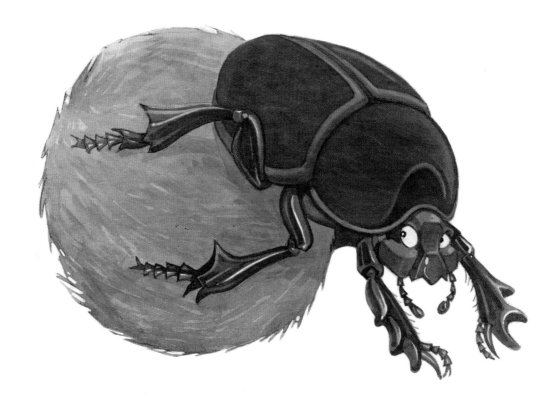

Insects Timeline

ca. 400 Million Years Ago

The first insects evolve. The oldest insect fossil we have today is 396 million years old. The insect looked a bit like a silverfish.

ca. 150 Million Years Ago

The giant insects that had scuttled through the prehistoric forests die out, leaving only the smaller insects we have now.

ca. 300 Million Years Ago

More modern-looking insects begin to appear—first beetles, then flies, and, 240 million years ago, wasps and moths.

ca. 4,000 Years Ago

Scarab beetles have godlike status in ancient Egypt, where they are linked with the Sun god, Ra.

1346–1353 CE

Rat fleas help carry the Black Death, killing up to half the population of Europe.

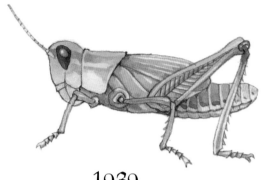

1939

Powerful insecticides are discovered, including DDT. They help to protect crops and control disease.

1970s

DDT is found to cause environmental damage and is widely banned.

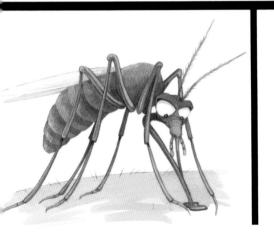

1897

Ronald Ross discovers that mosquitoes carry the malaria parasite.

Food Web

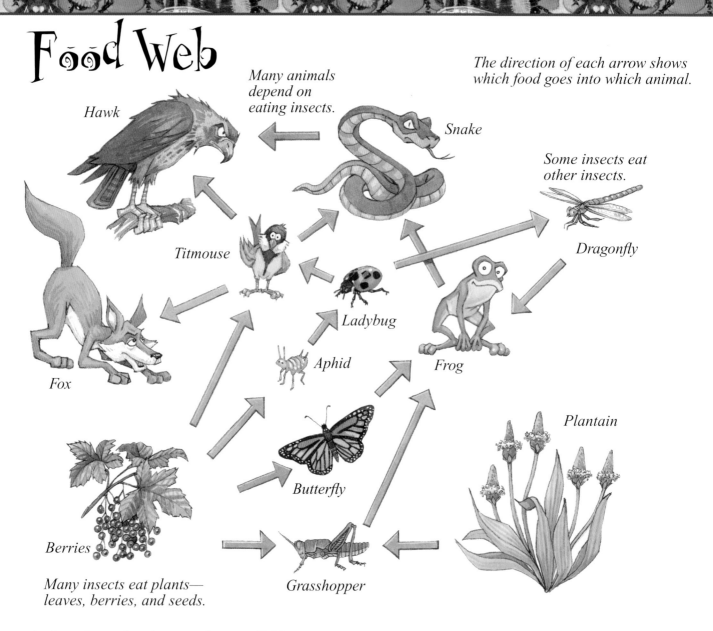

The direction of each arrow shows which food goes into which animal.

Many animals depend on eating insects.

Hawk

Snake

Some insects eat other insects.

Dragonfly

Titmouse

Ladybug

Frog

Fox

Aphid

Plantain

Butterfly

Berries

Many insects eat plants— leaves, berries, and seeds.

Grasshopper

A food web shows how different kinds of animals depend on each other for food. The plants at the bottom of the web are called primary producers. They take energy from the Sun, gases from the air, and nutrients from the soil to make the first type of food in the food web. Many insects and other animals eat plants. Then there are insects and other animals that eat plant-eating insects. Then more animals eat those. And when any plant or animal dies, insects eat it!

Author:

Anne Rooney studied English at Cambridge University, England, and then earned a PhD at Cambridge. She has held teaching posts at several UK universities and is currently a Royal Literary Fund fellow at Newnham College, Cambridge. She has written more than 150 books for children and adults, including several on the history of science and medicine. She also writes children's fiction.

Artist:

David Antram was born in Brighton, England, in 1958. He studied at Eastbourne College of Art and then worked in advertising for 15 years before becoming a full-time artist. He has illustrated many children's nonfiction books.

Series creator:

David Salariya was born in Dundee, Scotland. He has illustrated a wide range of books and has created and designed many new series for publishers in the UK and overseas. David established The Salariya Book Company in 1989. He lives in Brighton with his wife, illustrator Shirley Willis, and their son, Jonathan.

Editor: **Stephen Haynes**

Editorial Assistant: **Mark Williams**

PAPER FROM
SUSTAINABLE
FORESTS

Published in Great Britain in 2015 by
The Salariya Book Company Ltd
25 Marlborough Place, Brighton BN1 1UB

ISBN-13: 978-0-531-21362-9 (lib. bdg.) 978-0-531-21405-3 (pbk.)

All rights reserved.
Published in 2015 in the United States
by Franklin Watts
An imprint of Scholastic Inc.
Published simultaneously in Canada.

A CIP catalog record for this book is available
from the Library of Congress.

Printed and bound in China.
Printed on paper from sustainable sources.

1 2 3 4 5 6 7 8 9 10 R 24 23 22 21 20 19 18 17 16 15

SCHOLASTIC, FRANKLIN WATTS, and associated logos are
trademarks and/or registered trademarks of Scholastic Inc.

You Wouldn't Want to Live Without™
Insects!

Written by
Anne Rooney

Illustrated by
David Antram

Created and designed by
David Salariya

Franklin Watts®
An Imprint of Scholastic Inc.
NEW YORK • TORONTO • LONDON • AUCKLAND • SYDNEY
MEXICO CITY • NEW DELHI • HONG KONG
DANBURY, CONNECTICUT

Contents

Introduction

You might think it would be rather nice to live in a world without insects. There would be no wasps to sting you, no mosquitoes to bite you, no ants to crawl over your picnic, and no annoying head lice to make your head itch. Your dog wouldn't get fleas and your plants wouldn't be eaten by aphids. It all sounds nice and peaceful, doesn't it? Insects can be real pests, and we often go to a lot of trouble to kill them.

But not all insects are pests. And many of them are a lot more helpful to us than you might think—even insects you might not like! Without insects, we would have a lot less to eat. The world would get really messy, too. They might be small, but some insects do big, important jobs!

So, don't use this book to swat a fly—read on and find out just how useful insects can be. And then decide: would you *really* want to live in a world without insects?

Zzzzzzzz

You little pest!

INSECTS have been on Earth a lot longer than we have. They got here first—so give them a bit of a break!

Insects Rule!

You could have found insects in a prehistoric swamp if you'd been around then. Insects are arthropods, and arthropods were the first type of animal to come out of the water and live on land, about 450 million years ago. Arthropods include spiders, crabs, scorpions, centipedes, and millipedes, as well as insects. The first insects appeared on Earth around 400 million years ago—and they've been here ever since.

A while after insects first appeared, they grew and grew and grew until they were pretty big. Luckily for us, the biggest insects died out around 150 million years ago.

DINOSAURS had their own troubles with insects. Fleas up to ten times the size of modern fleas must have made them itch. Some scientists think diseases carried by insects helped to kill off the dinosaurs.

Stegosaurus and flea, ca. 155–150 million years ago

Giant insects and other arthropods, ca. 300–200 million years ago

THE LARGEST insects to exist thrived in the Paleozoic era, which ended 250 million years ago. The giant dragonfly *Meganeura* had a wingspan up to 25.5 inches (65 centimeters). That's longer than your arm!

You Can Do It!

Next time you're outside, see how many types of insects you can find. Look on the ground, on walls, in the sky, on plants, under stones, in rotting wood... But if you live in an area where dangerous things could be lurking, be careful!

WE'RE OUTNUMBERED! There are 200 million insects for every person on Earth. That's 200 million for you, 200 million for me...

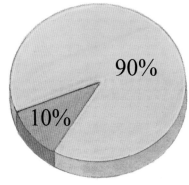

90%

10%

MADE TO MEASURE There are specialized insects adapted to feeding on all types of plants and animals—nothing is safe! And insects are found on land everywhere in the world—even in frozen Antarctica.

INSECTS are really successful. There are 6 to 10 million species, though scientists have only named about 900,000 species. Around 90 percent of all life-forms on Earth, not counting bacteria, are insects.

IT'S NOT JUST NUMBERS. The mass of all the ants in the world is greater than the mass of all the people. In a rain forest, insects weigh more than all the vertebrates (animals with backbones) added together.

How Insects Work

nsects are tiny but tough. They have their hard parts on the outside, like a suit of armor. They can put up with harsh conditions, too, and survive far better than other animals when the going gets tough. Cockroaches can live for six weeks without any food—and four weeks without a head! Wasps can survive 180 times as much radiation as we can. After a nuclear explosion at Chernobyl, Ukraine, in 1986, insects survived better than other animals. Insects are often the first creatures to move back into a disaster zone.

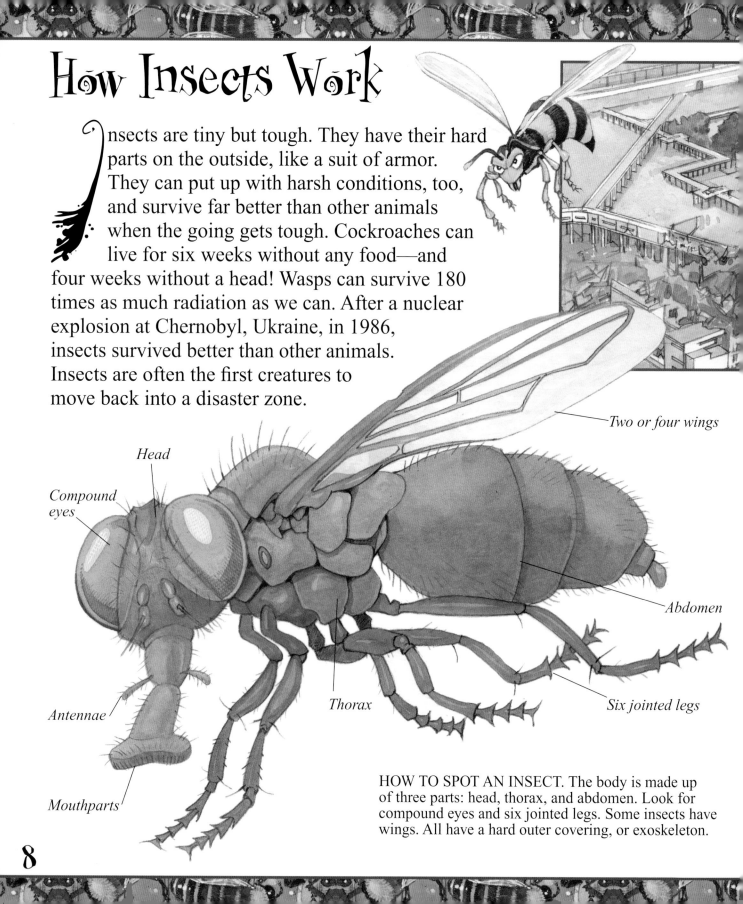

Two or four wings

Head

Compound eyes

Abdomen

Antennae

Thorax

Six jointed legs

Mouthparts

HOW TO SPOT AN INSECT. The body is made up of three parts: head, thorax, and abdomen. Look for compound eyes and six jointed legs. Some insects have wings. All have a hard outer covering, or exoskeleton.

CHERNOBYL NUCLEAR POWER PLANT. In a hostile environment, wasps, cockroaches, and termites are more likely to survive than larger animals with soft bodies.

You Can Do It!

See like an insect! You can make your own compound eye by gathering up a bunch of drinking straws and looking through them all together. Cut them short to make it easier.

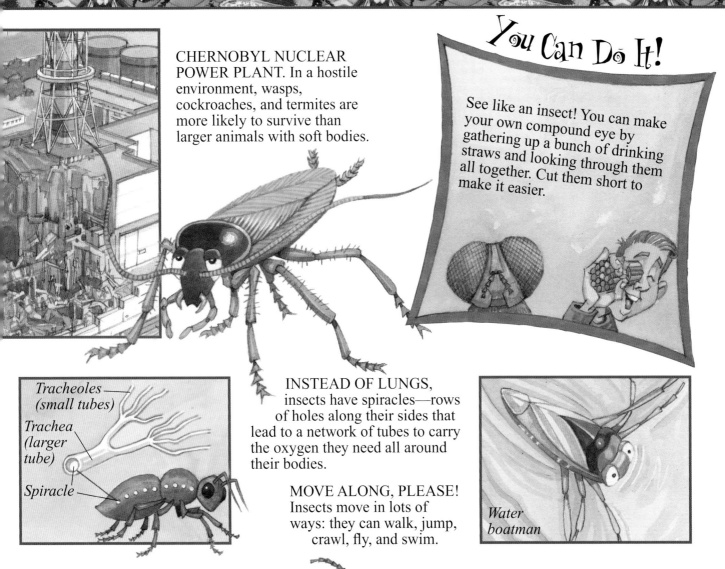

Tracheoles (small tubes)

Trachea (larger tube)

Spiracle

INSTEAD OF LUNGS, insects have spiracles—rows of holes along their sides that lead to a network of tubes to carry the oxygen they need all around their bodies.

MOVE ALONG, PLEASE! Insects move in lots of ways: they can walk, jump, crawl, fly, and swim.

Water boatman

DINNERTIME! Insects have different types of mouths for eating different sorts of food. Ants have snipping, chewing mandibles to cut up plant matter or meat. Butterflies have a long tongue for taking nectar from inside flowers. Flies have a tubelike mouth; they spill saliva (spit) on their food to dissolve it and then suck it up. Bees have a lapping tongue to suck up nectar.

Ant

Butterfly

Fly

Bee

INSECTS eat plants, dead animals, rotting food, and dung. Dragonfly larvae (right) even eat small fish!

Insect Life Cycles

You were born as a fully formed human being and have just kept growing bigger since then. Insects don't have such an easy time. Most go through at least four very different life stages.

They start as an egg, laid near a source of food so that they don't have to move far when they hatch. The egg hatches into a larva. The larval stage of some insects has a special name, such as "caterpillar" or "maggot." The larva moves around, feeding and growing. When it's large enough, it makes a cocoon and turns into a pupa. The pupa doesn't move, but changes go on inside it. At last, the fully formed insect emerges from the pupa and flies, creeps, or scuttles away.

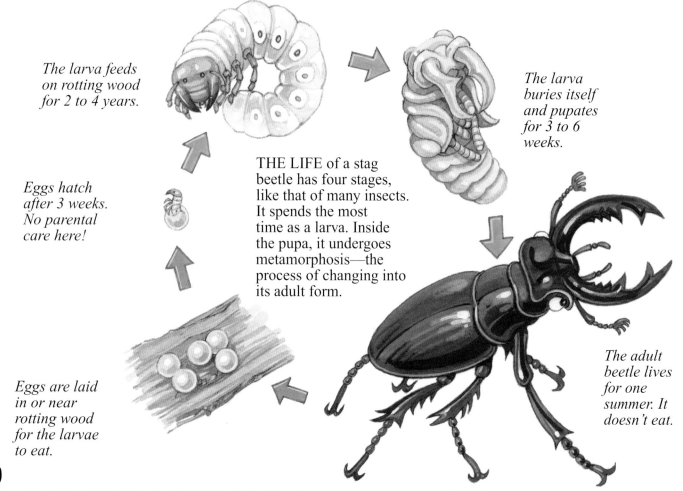

The larva feeds on rotting wood for 2 to 4 years.

The larva buries itself and pupates for 3 to 6 weeks.

Eggs hatch after 3 weeks. No parental care here!

THE LIFE of a stag beetle has four stages, like that of many insects. It spends the most time as a larva. Inside the pupa, it undergoes metamorphosis—the process of changing into its adult form.

Eggs are laid in or near rotting wood for the larvae to eat.

The adult beetle lives for one summer. It doesn't eat.

DURING METAMORPHOSIS, the insect doesn't move around or eat—it just changes into a different form. When it comes out, it's fully grown.

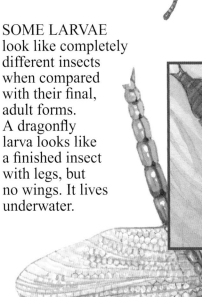

LADYBUG larvae are bigger than the ladybugs they eventually turn into. You can often find them on stinging nettles.

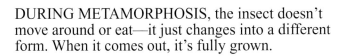

You Can Do It!

Find a caterpillar. Without touching the caterpillar, put it in a glass jar. Add the same type of leaves you found it on. Make holes in the lid to let in air. Add fresh leaves until the caterpillar turns into a pupa. When it starts emerging, release it immediately. Be careful if you live in an area with dangerous insects!

SOME LARVAE look like completely different insects when compared with their final, adult forms. A dragonfly larva looks like a finished insect with legs, but no wings. It lives underwater.

Nymphs

SOME INSECTS have only three stages: egg, nymph, and adult. A locust goes through five nymph stages called instars. It has to shed its hard skin as it grows, because the skin can't stretch.

Big, Bad Bugs

Some insects can bite, sting, suck your blood, or give you diseases. No wonder people don't like them!

And some of the diseases spread by insects are really nasty. Today, the biggest threat is malaria, a tropical disease that causes terrible fever. It kills 700,000 to 1.2 million people a year. Malaria is caused by a tiny parasite that lives part of its life cycle in the gut of the mosquito and part in the liver and blood of humans. When a mosquito carrying the parasite bites a person, the parasites move into the person.

ONLY THE *ANOPHELES* mosquito carries the malaria parasite—and only the female mosquitoes bite. Males eat nectar, so they can't hurt you. Malaria doesn't hurt the mosquito; it only hurts us.

Whine Whine Whine

It could be our turn next.

RAT FLEAS probably helped spread the plague, or Black Death, in the 1340s. The bacteria that cause bubonic plague can be carried from rats to humans by flea bites.

Top Tip

If you live in an area where biting insects are a problem, protect yourself! Sleeping under a mosquito net, or with nets over the windows, is a good way to prevent bites at night. It's the main protection against malaria.

Head louse

THE DROPPINGS of an assassin bug can carry parasites that cause Chagas disease. If you scratch the bite, the parasites can get into your blood. Chagas disease can cause life-threatening damage.

SOME INSECTS have a sharp stinger at the tail end. Only female wasps have a stinger, developed from the egg-laying tube. You might not want to get close enough to check, though.

HEAD LICE are tiny, biting insects you may be familiar with. They lay their eggs at the base of a hair. When they hatch, they bite your scalp to suck blood. Allergy to the lice makes your head itch.

13

Exterminate!

Some insects can do massive damage and are real pests. They can wreck crops and buildings, and even make areas of land unusable by humans.

People who live in areas plagued by locusts might think they would be happy to live in a world without insects! Vast swarms of hundreds of billions of locusts darken the sky as they devour all the vegetation in their path. Each locust eats its own weight in food every day. A single swarm can cover 460 square miles (1,200 square kilometers), destroying crops and causing famine.

WOODWORM are beetle larvae. Adult beetles lay eggs in wood—including floorboards, beams, and furniture—and the larvae munch away at the wood when they hatch.

Crumble

My favorite sweater!

THE LARVAE of clothes moths feast on fabrics, ruining clothes, carpets, and furnishings. They especially like to munch on natural fibers, and wool is their favorite.

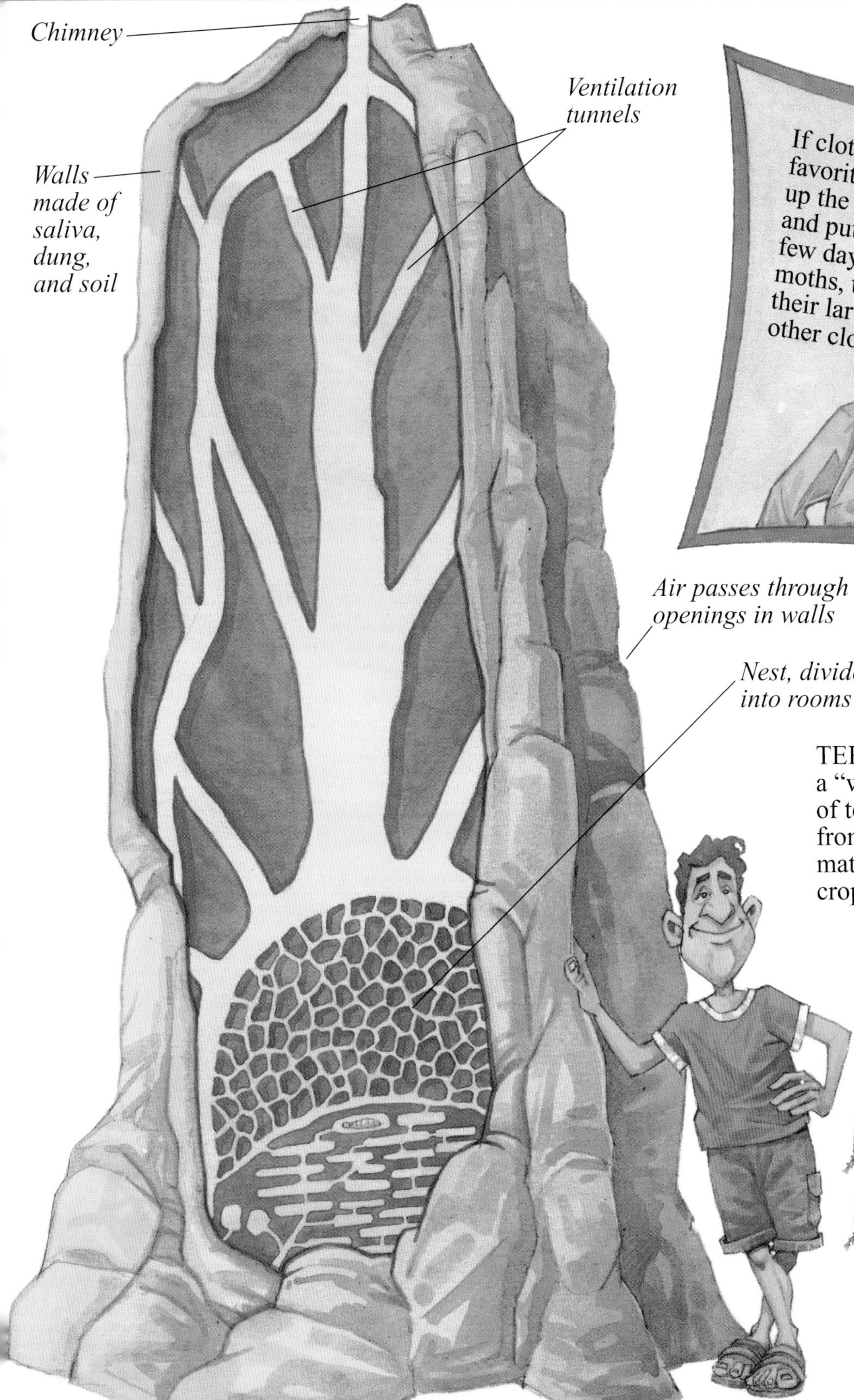

Chimney

Ventilation tunnels

Walls made of saliva, dung, and soil

Top Tip

If clothes moths attack your favorite sweater or jacket, wrap up the item in a plastic bag and put it in the freezer for a few days. That should kill the moths, their eggs, and their larvae. Check your other clothes, too!

Air passes through openings in walls

Nest, divided into rooms

TERMITES look like ants without a "waist." Colonies of millions of termites make towering nests from chewed-up wood and plant material—including chewed-up crops and wooden buildings.

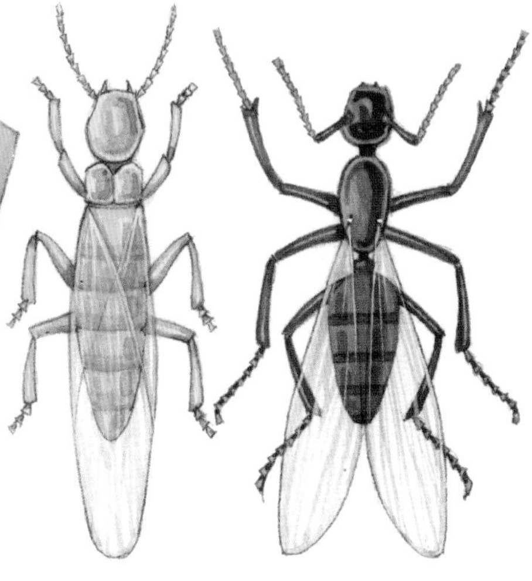

Termite   Flying ant

15

Destruction Is Good!

Although it's a nuisance if insects eat your sweater, your house, or your crops, the destructive behavior of insects is vital to keep the world going. Who do you think gets rid of all the plants and animals that die? Who clears up all the dung that animals drop?

Insects are the great recyclers. They break up dead things and dung, and they eat this refuse, lay eggs in it, or drag it underground where bacteria get to work on it. Without the insect scavengers, the world would disappear under a mountain of waste of the nastiest kind.

KANGAROO DUNG is neat and dry. Cow dung is sloppy and messy. When people first took cows to Australia, the dung beetles couldn't cope with cow dung. The mess built up—at a rate of 12 million cow pies an hour! Special dung beetles were imported from Africa to clean up.

DEAD ANIMALS and plants make a meal for lots of insects. Many types of flies and beetles lay eggs in dead flesh. When the maggots hatch, they munch away on the meat, tidying up.

FORENSIC ENTOMOLOGISTS are experts who can tell how long a body has been dead and where it has been from the insects living in it. They help police solve violent crimes.

Aha!

How It Works

When an animal dies, bacteria and chemicals inside it start to break up the tissue. From the outside, insects eat parts of the body and lay their eggs in it. The eggs hatch into larvae which feed on the body, too. Different insects are attracted at different stages— some like fresh meat, and some like it old and rotting.

SOME ADULT DUNG BEETLES roll a ball of dung and lay their eggs inside. When the larvae hatch, guess what they eat…

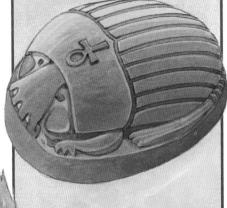

Ancient Egyptian carving of a scarab beetle

SCARAB BEETLES are dung beetles, and there are over 30,000 types. The ancient Egyptians realized how useful they were and worshipped them. They even mummified them!

Bugs Make the World Go Around

nsects buzzing around your summer picnic might be annoying, but you wouldn't have the picnic at all if there were no insects! Three-quarters of the world's plants and a third of all crops are pollinated by animals, and most of those useful animals are insects. Without them, we wouldn't have any fruit or flowers and we'd have far fewer vegetables. Even if you don't like eating vegetables, other animals do—and you might want to eat those animals, or drink their milk.

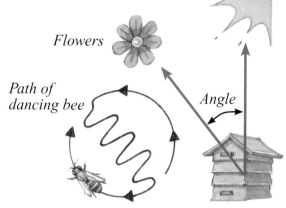

A BEE that has found flowers tells other bees where to find them by doing a "waggle dance." The dance shows the direction as an angle with the Sun as well as showing the distance to the flowers.

THERE ARE LOTS OF FOODS we wouldn't have if it weren't for insects, such as onions, peppers, cocoa, cabbage, broccoli, beans, coffee, grapes, strawberries, apples, and pears.

A BEE feeding on nectar picks up pollen on its legs. When it flies to another flower, the pollen is brushed off and pollinates the flower, which then makes seeds.

Pistil receives pollen from bees

Anthers (tips of stamens) produce pollen

Ovary (where seeds are produced)

Pollen

Save the Bees!

Bees are in danger around the world. Modern farming methods have destroyed diverse habitats, and insecticides kill bees. Bees can also fall sick and die from diseases or parasites. If the bees die out, we will face disaster. A world without bees would see widespread famine.

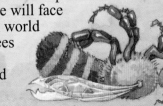

Bad Guys Turn Good

Some insects are pests at one stage in their lives, but useful to humans in another stage. They might eat crops as larvae but pollinate crops as adults. Or they might remove waste as larvae but become pesky pests as adults.

There are lots of ways of being useful. Insects are useful food for people in some parts of the world.

And many are useful food for other animals. Many fish, reptiles, mammals, and birds eat insects, their larvae, or their eggs, and some of those animals are themselves useful food sources for humans.

But the very same insects that are useful food sources can also be a nuisance, eating our crops, carrying diseases, or undermining buildings and other structures. Good guys can be bad, and bad guys can be good!

WHEN THE CATERPILLARS HATCH, they chomp away at the cabbage. That's pretty annoying if you're a cabbage farmer.

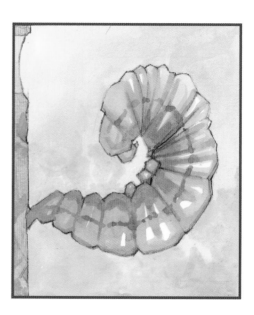

BY THE TIME the caterpillar is ready to pupate, it's usually done a lot of damage to the cabbage.

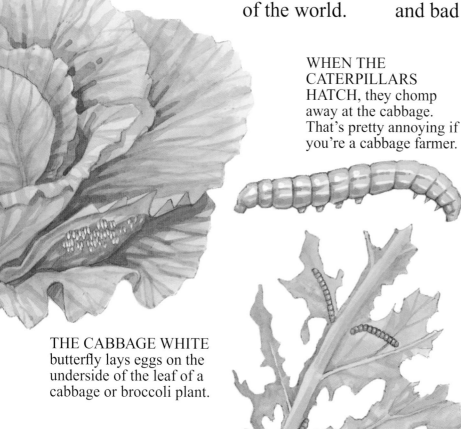

THE CABBAGE WHITE butterfly lays eggs on the underside of the leaf of a cabbage or broccoli plant.

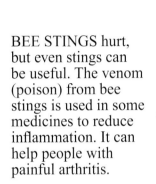

YOU MIGHT NOT THINK there's anything good about wasps. But they eat lots of other insects and their larvae, including caterpillars that destroy crops. So they're not all bad!

BEE STINGS hurt, but even stings can be useful. The venom (poison) from bee stings is used in some medicines to reduce inflammation. It can help people with painful arthritis.

You Can Do It!

Sit quietly by a flower bed or a flowering tree. After a while, you may see insects come to collect nectar. As they crawl over the flowers, pollen sticks to their bodies. You may be able to see it as yellow dust.

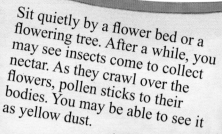

WHEN THE BUTTERFLY EMERGES, it's ready to be useful. It doesn't eat any more cabbage—now it pollinates flowers. If we got rid of all the caterpillars, who would do the pollinating?

ANT BITES aren't nice. But some societies have used ants to "stitch" wounds closed. People make the ant bite through the edges of the wound, then snap off the body, leaving the head and pincers in place.

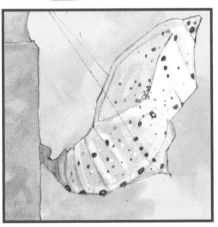

21

Insects in Science

Humans have found insects useful in some unusual ways, too. Their ways of moving and working together have given scientists ideas for ways of moving and controlling robots.

Many insects, such as locusts, ants, and bees, work together in a swarm. They communicate, cooperate, and share tasks—just as you are told to do at school. Scientists have learned useful tricks from them. And fruit flies are used in genetics research, because they grow and breed so quickly.

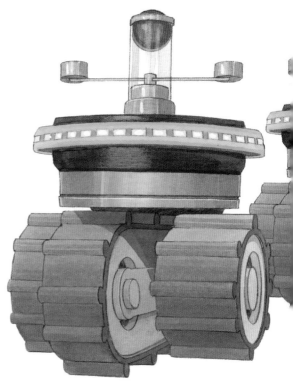

COCKROACHES can scurry into tiny spaces. Fitted with electronic backpacks that can control their movements or take videos, they could play a vital role in rescue work.

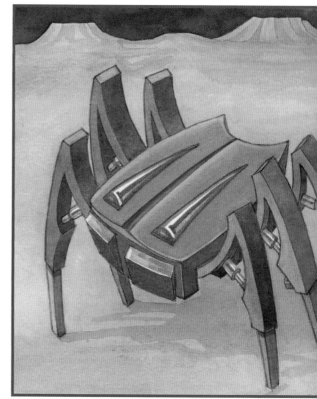

In ant and bee colonies, different groups have different functions and body designs—some are workers that build the swarm's home, some collect food, some reproduce or look after young. Swarming insects communicate with each other to locate food and warn of danger.

SWARMING behavior has been copied to make swarmbots (above)—robots that act together to carry out shared tasks such as searching, sensing, or maintenance activities.

Bug one to Mission Control...

MOVING OVER a difficult landscape is easier with legs than wheels (left). Some prototype rovers for exploring other planets move in the same way as crawling insects. Some can even transform their legs into wheels when they reach flatter ground.

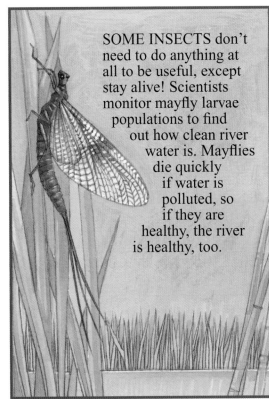

SOME INSECTS don't need to do anything at all to be useful, except stay alive! Scientists monitor mayfly larvae populations to find out how clean river water is. Mayflies die quickly if water is polluted, so if they are healthy, the river is healthy, too.

23

Industrious Insects

Some insects make things that people can use—that's a lot better than destroying things we've already made.

Bees make honey and beeswax, which we take from them and use. (Don't worry: They make more than they need.) They collect nectar from flowers and make it into honey, which they store in a honeycomb—a wax structure of hexagonal cells. The bees keep the honey to feed the hive in the winter. Beekeepers gather the honey from hives—carefully!

Beehive

Bees fly 55,000 miles to make a pound of honey!*

Frame containing honeycomb

* That's nearly 200,000 km to make 1 kg.

BEESWAX from the honeycomb is used to make candles and wax polish.

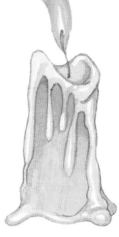

HONEY is made by bees taking nectar into their honey stomach and then regurgitating it back at the hive. Other bees chew it and spit it out. So, would you like some bee vomit on that toast?

How It Works

The silkworm makes silk from its own spit, which hardens in the air into a fiber. Usually the pupa is killed and the cocoon unwound, but cruelty-free silk is made by letting the silkworms hatch. The fiber is broken by the emerging moth, so the silk has to be spun from short threads.

Making Silk

SILK is made from the very thin fibers of the silkworm's cocoon. It takes 3,000 silkworms to make 2.2 pounds (1 kilogram) of silk. The larvae feed on mulberry leaves (left) until they are ready to pupate.

THE SILKWORM spins a single strand of silk that it winds around and around itself to make a cocoon (right). The strand is up to 0.9 miles (1.5 km) long and 0.0005 inches (13 microns) thick.

THE PUPAE are baked to kill the larvae, then boiled to loosen the silk. A skilled silk worker finds the end of the thread (left) and uses a machine to help unwind the long thread from each cocoon.

IN SOME COUNTRIES, the pupae from inside the cocoons are considered a tasty meal (right). You can buy them in tins.

Eat and Be Eaten

Even insects that we don't think are useful to us are important in the food chain. Ecosystems are carefully balanced, and insects are both consumers and food—eaters and eaten.

Some insects eat others that are pests to humans. They help to control bugs that gobble up our crops or cause other types of harm. A ladybug will eat 50 aphids a day, and a ladybug larva eats its own weight in aphids each day. Farmers can even buy in insects to help control crop pests, instead of using chemical pesticides.

Many animals that we like to encourage eat insects. Frogs and birds eat insects, and also eat other garden pests such as snails.

FROGS EAT lots of different types of insects. The frog's sticky tongue flicks out at lightning speed to pick up a passing fly or beetle. A frog will eat thousands over the course of its life.

A LACEWING larva eats aphids, caterpillars, mites, insect eggs, and all kinds of pests. In Australia, farmers introduce them to rapeseed crops (plants used to make animal feed and vegetable oil) specifically to eat pests.

ANTS MAKE GOOD FARMERS—they farm aphids! That makes them unpopular with gardeners, though, as they keep the aphids alive and don't stop them eating plants. The ants "milk" the aphids for their juices.

IT'S NOT JUST other animals that eat insects. In some parts of the world, insects are an important part of the human diet. If locusts eat your crop, you might as well eat the locusts!

Tŏp Tĭp

If you don't like the idea of eating insects, be grateful that you're not a pangolin, or scaly anteater. They eat up to 7 ounces (200 grams) of insects a day—mostly ants and termites.

You don't know what you're missing!

INSECTS AREN'T always good for you. Sometimes they come in a sugar lollipop or dipped in chocolate. These are just as bad for you as any other sweets!

THE LARVAE of some types of insects are eaten as a snack, in soups and stews, or fried. In some places, you can buy them as street food on sticks. They can be a delicacy.

Good, Bad, and Ugly Bugs

If we didn't try to limit populations of some insects, the world would be wracked by famine, disease, and destruction. But if we wiped them out completely, then the world would be wracked by famine, disease, and piles of waste. Insects are part of the complicated ecological jigsaw puzzle and we disrupt it at our peril.

In the 1940s and 1950s, a new insecticide called DDT was widely used. By killing mosquitoes and controlling malaria, it saved millions of lives. But DDT got into the food chain, killing birds and animals that eat insects. Its use is now tightly controlled, and safer, more ecologically aware methods are used to keep insect populations balanced. We don't want too many insects—but we can't live without them.

A BAT CAN EAT up to 3,000 insects a night. In the 1900s, a doctor in Texas, Charles Campbell, built bat-roosting towers to lure hungry bats to eat malaria-carrying mosquitoes.

SCIENTISTS have tried for years to breed mosquitoes that can't carry malaria or can't breed, so that the natural mosquitoes could be displaced by them.

You Can Do It!

Insects are good for your garden, but as we destroy more of their natural homes, they are finding life harder. You can make a nesting area or winter hideaway to help them out. Pile up tubes, pots, hollow canes, and anything else they can crawl into to sleep safely.

Bamboo canes

Flowerpots   *Flat stones*

Logs

The Four Pests

IN 1958, China launched a campaign to kill off four pests—rats, mosquitoes, flies, and sparrows. It was disastrous, as the role of these "pests" in nature wasn't properly understood. People killed sparrows because the birds ate crops. But insects ate even more crops. With no birds to eat insects, the insects ate everything, causing a famine.

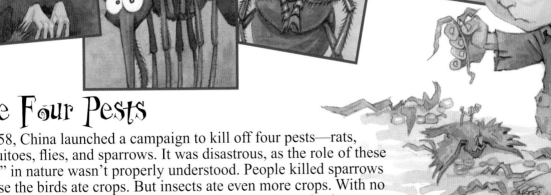

Glossary

Abdomen An insect's third body section (tail end) that contains the organs for digestion and reproduction.

Allergy A response of the body to a substance that seems to be a threat. An allergy might make you sneeze, itch, get spots, go red, or struggle to breathe.

Arthritis A painful condition in which the joints are damaged and swollen.

Arthropod An animal with a hard exoskeleton, a body divided into segments, and jointed legs.

Bacteria (singular: **bacterium**) Single-celled microorganisms. Some types cause disease; others are harmless or even helpful.

Cocoon A case that an insect makes around itself at the end of the larval stage. Inside, the insect becomes a pupa and changes into the adult form.

Compound eye An eye composed of lots of tiny eye units all working together. It gives a wide field of vision and good perception of movement, but provides less detail than simple eyes.

Ecological Relating to the interactions between animals and plants and their environment.

Ecosystem A community of organisms living together in an environment.

Entomologist A scientist who studies insects.

Exoskeleton The hard outer casing that serves instead of bones to keep the bodies of insects and other arthropods rigid.

Famine An extreme shortage of food, leading to people starving.

Forensic Relating to the use of science in criminal investigations.

Genetics The study of how organisms inherit characteristics from their parents.

Infection A disease or illness caused by the action of a microorganism.

Inflammation A painful, red swelling of part of the body as a response to illness or damage.

Insecticide A chemical that kills insects.

Larva The first stage of an organism (such as an insect) that goes through different stages as it grows. The larva is the form that hatches from the egg.

Metamorphosis The way an organism changes from one form to another, such as a tadpole changing into a frog.

Microorganism A living organism usually too small to see with the naked eye but visible through a microscope.

Mummified Preserved after death by using chemicals and wrapping techniques to stop a body decaying.

Nectar A sugary syrup produced by flowers to attract insects.

Nymph An early stage in the life cycle of some insects and other animals.

Organism Any living being, such as a plant, animal, or fungus.

Parasite An organism that lives on or in another one, and takes food from it.

Plague A deadly disease caused by the bacterium *Yersinia pestis*.

Pollen A yellow or orange powder produced by flowers that contains the male (sperm) cells needed to combine with female cells to make seeds.

Pollinate To move pollen between flowers so that the flowers can produce seeds.

Prototype A working, trial design for a new product.

Pupa A stage in the development of an organism in which it changes from a larva to the adult form.

Thorax The middle part of an insect's body, between the head and abdomen.

Vertebrate An animal with a backbone.

Index

How to Spot Non-Insects

We often use the word *bug* to refer to all kinds of arthropods, but not all arthropods are insects. You might come across any of these non-insects around your house, garden, or school.

Spiders have eight legs and a body divided into only two parts (head and abdomen, no thorax)— that's two more legs and one fewer body parts than an insect. Some spiders are very dangerous. If there are dangerous spiders where you live, don't go looking for them!

Centipedes have long bodies divided into segments, and one pair of legs on each segment. *Centipede* means "100 feet," but no centipede actually has 100 feet. They all have an odd number of pairs of legs—so a centipede could have 98 legs (49 pairs) or 102 legs (51 pairs). They can have fewer than 20 or more than 300 legs.

Millipedes ("1,000 feet") have two pairs of legs on each body segment, but none has more than 750 legs in all.

Pill bugs, or roly polies, are crustaceans, like prawns, lobsters, and crabs. They have fourteen legs and a segmented body with a hard exoskeleton that they shed and replace as they grow. They live in dark, damp places where they eat rotting wood and plant matter. Some pill bugs can roll into a ball when alarmed.

Top Record-Breaking Insects

Fastest
A dragonfly that reaches speeds of 35 miles per hour (56 kph) is the fastest known insect.

Largest
The giant weta of New Zealand, which looks like a cricket, is the largest insect in the world. The biggest known weta weighed 2.5 ounces (71 g) and was 3.3 inches (8.5 cm) long, not counting its legs and antennae.

Smallest
A type of fairyfly from Costa Rica is only 0.0055 inches, or five and a half thousandths of an inch (0.14 mm) long. That's no bigger than some single-celled organisms!

Most Adventurous
The globe skimmer, which looks like a dragonfly, migrates during the rainy season from India to south or east Africa and back—a journey of up to 11,000 miles (18,000 km).

Most Painful
The worst insect bite is inflicted by the bullet ant. The bite is so painful it feels like a gunshot (that's why it's called a bullet ant). But it's not dangerous. If you're bitten, it hurts for up to 24 hours and then you get better.

Most Mysterious
The giant willow aphid may be the largest aphid of all, but very little is known about it. In February, all willow aphids disappear for five months. No one knows where they go. And no male willow aphid has ever been found. The females clone themselves, making exact copies without ever mating.

Did You Know?

- A termite queen can lay 20,000 to 30,000 eggs a day and can live for 45 years. That's between a third of a billion and half a billion eggs over her lifetime!

- Prehistoric insects could grow so large because there was more oxygen in the atmosphere then. We couldn't have giant insects now, because the simple breathing system that insects have cannot cope well with lower amounts of oxygen.

- Scientists have produced a silkworm with a spider gene that produces superstrong silk. Spider silk is as strong as steel, but spiders can't be farmed. Getting silkworms to make spider silk is the perfect solution, because they're easy to farm.

- Farmers can rent hives of bees to pollinate their crops. They can also buy fly larvae that have parasitic wasp eggs laid inside them. The wasps hatch and infect other flies, helping control pests on the farm.

- The skin of a larva such as a caterpillar or silkworm doesn't stretch. As the larva grows, its skin gets tighter until it has to molt, shedding the too-small outer skin and growing a new one.

- Not all bees live in hives. Some are solitary. And some solitary bees lay their eggs in empty snail shells—the ultimate recycling of homes!

- Tomato plants are pollinated mainly by bumblebees, as they need the buzzing, vibrating movement of the bumblebee. If you try to grow tomato plants and no bumblebees come, you can use an old electric toothbrush (not one you use for your teeth!) as a "bee" and pollinate the flowers yourself.